"As much of a recovery memoir as it is a practical guidebook for successfully rebuilding yourself from the wreckage. With his first book, King doesn't simply strip recovery down to its bones. No, he hands you a blueprint, shows you where to hang the scaffolding, loans you his toolbelt, and then proves that you can accomplish something that might otherwise seem impossible. In many ways, King's book is a remarkable feat: it renders recovery as a straightforward process, but no less a miracle in and of itself."– **Paul Fuhr, author of "Bottleneck" and creator of the podcast "Drop the Needle"**

In loving memory of my friend Max
and cousin Amber

Table of Contents

So, what is a proud addict?

To me being a proud addict is something that gave my whole life a new perspective when it came to my recovery. Being proud of who you are and what you choose to be is something that I never really found when I was searching for new ways to deal with my addiction. Being told that this is something that I was going to have to deal with my entire life was something that I refused to take as a negative thing.

I attempted sobriety many times before with no success, going up to 3 months at a time before I would again relapse. I felt that recovery was hopeless and was devastated that I had to fight this the rest of my life. I thought to myself many times "Why can't I just be a normal person? Why do I have to live such a hard life?". It wasn't until my fourth time trying recovery that my perspective would change, and I would start to see things in a new light. Right then and there I refused to see my life as a mistake. I refused to live a life of negativity and live in remorse of my addiction. I was given this illness, but I would not let it bring me down. It was time for me to choose nothing other than to believe in myself and be proud of who I am.

Addiction is not a death sentence. Addiction is not something that labels you as a bad person. Addicts are some of the strongest people in the world and I know that we deserve that feeling.

What makes an addict strong is their honesty and ability to adapt to life changing events that may make others crumble. For those of you who do not understand addiction and how it works, try this. Think and write down on a piece of paper what the most important things in your life are. These things are commonly your children, family, hobbies, etc. Now take that paper and rip it to shreds because those things are not good for you and you can't be around them anymore. This is how an addict's mind feels when they are told they can no longer use their drug of choice. This seems dramatic, but our brains are wired to make us feel that we cannot live without this drug and that it needs to be the first thing we focus on for the day.

This overwhelming urge powered by our brains is what makes us do things that a normal person wouldn't. No child says they want to be an addict when they grow up and becoming an addict is nothing that is planned. No addict wants to ruin their lives, and unfortunately once we realize what our actions are doing, we are already so deep into our active addiction that it seems impossible to get out off. That's why when someone chooses to get into recovery it really is truly remarkable. It is the stereotype that people with an addiction are bad people that is keeping addicts from choosing to be in recovery. If you think about it, why would you try and change your life if you are going to be looked down upon even if you have a large amount of time in recovery? This is exactly why I chose to change my perspective for my recovery and my addiction.

I refused to let anyone tell me I wasn't a strong person and that I wasn't meant to do great things. Overcoming active addiction is no doubt one of the hardest things to do in life but it is an amazing gift of gratitude that I am so proud to have. I am happy that I am an addict. I am proud to be able to show the world that it is possible to bring yourself back from the darkest of places and live every minute to the fullest truly grateful to be alive. I know that every day I will have to fight my addiction to prove that I am strong and that truly is something that I look forward to everyday. If I did not have my addiction, I would not feel the amount of extreme gratitude of every day having another day of being sober and alive. I have now been sober for over 5 years and I can honestly say that every single day in recovery has been better than the last. That is something that I never want to lose.

This is why I consider myself to be a proud addict and that I couldn't be happier with the challenges my life has thrown my way. This is not a book of the 12 steps, I wrote this book to provide a chance for you to find a new and more positive outlook on our lives as addicts. No matter if you have been sober for 20 years or are just starting your recovery today, today is the beginning of your new life and you deserve the best.

Do you want to be sober?

If you are not sure if you want to be sober, I can tell you right now that you are ready to start your life of sobriety. You just might not believe it yet. Our subconscious has been there from our very first use of our drug of choice telling us "This isn't a good idea" or "You really shouldn't be doing this" and has never left. We are just good, and pretty much experts, on ignoring it. Now is the time to start your life of becoming a confident and proud person of your recovery and everything that it can bring to your life.

Open your mind to this new perspective of seeing addiction as a gift and I can promise you that your life will become something you never thought it could be. Your life can be accelerated by the unexpected and eye-opening world of successful recovery.

CHAPTER 1

The Time Travel Perspective

we are the ones who are going to be the most honest with ourselves over anyone else.

"If I could go back, I would have changed so many things", "Man, if I would have just done this I would have been in such a better place right now", "Your lucky you're still young because I would love to be that young again".

These are all things that we have heard or said probably a hundred times. All of the wishing we have done reflecting on the past, just expecting that our mistakes have created our destiny. I guess there's nothing we can do now right? Wrong! We need to keep things in perspective that yes, time does seem to go by very fast, but we still have so much time left to make some big changes in our lives. I think this perspective is the most beneficial to start your journey into recovery and understanding the mentality of being a proud addict. So, read carefully and take this perspective to heart.

This perspective is mainly focused on long term goal setting and figuring out what small goals we can set to reach them. The idea is to put yourself into a mindset of meeting yourself sometime in the future and being honest about what they would tell you to do today in the present.

Put yourself in your own mindset 1 year from now. What would they be happy about you starting today? This is where the "Time Travel" comes into play for the time travel perspective.

We often find ourselves living in the past making wishes of things we didn't do or wish we had started. There is no benefit in this other than to find out those wishes are something we can work on now, which undoubtably happens to every person anywhere. I emphasize what you specifically would tell yourself a year from now because *we are the ones who are going to be the most honest with ourselves over anyone else*. We know better than anyone else what we are capable of and what we honestly want in this life therefore we have all the potential of being our best motivator.

When my clients ask me for advice about what coping skills they can use, I give them the basics like having someone to trust, taking a long walk when you feel a trigger coming on and calling me, even if it is just to leave a message saying that you are having a trigger. Sometimes just verbalizing out loud what you are facing can be very therapeutic. Once I give them those basic coping skills, I then tell them that they are the ones who are going to find out what coping skills will help them out the most. I always tell them that they are their best counselor. You are your best counselor. I say this because you can tell anyone anything you want, but whether you believe that or not is between only you and yourself.

This is why consulting and imagining what you know you would tell you a year from now is the most beneficial way to set your long-term goals. You know yourself better than anyone, so make that decision to be your best self and be honest about what you know you can achieve. This is what the time travel perspective is all about.

Trust your struggle

A lot of the time when we are setting goals we only focus on the feeling of when the goal is achieved. When we do this, we are taking away a decent amount of the enjoyment of goal setting. When we only focus on the end goal and do not focus on the dedication that we are putting into reaching that goal, we sell ourselves short of reaching that goal every day.

When I say this, I mean that with every goal that we have in mind we know what we need to do to achieve it. So, if your goal is to graduate college, if your homework is done you achieved that long-term goal for the day. Learning to love and be proud of the work you are doing the whole time you are doing it is what is going to help you most in your recovery.

Don't wait for the satisfaction of your goal being set. Be satisfied about the hard work that you are doing to achieve it. Embrace your inner warrior and bring it to light. *Trust your struggle because your struggle means you are moving in the right direction.*

CHAPTER 2

One Day At A Time

*there is a reason that cliché sayings are
so common. It's because they work*

The commonly used phrase in both recovery and stress relieving aspects of life is taking it "One Day at a Time". This no doubt falls under the category of a cliché saying but there is a reason that cliché sayings are so common. *It's because they work.* That being said I think my perspective on 'one day at a time' can give you an opportunity to see it in a different light.

One day at a time is something that can seem hard to do at first and seem like it's a totally different way of life. In all reality, we have been practicing it everyday in our active addiction. I know that when I got up everyday in my active addiction, I had no interest in tomorrow, I only worried about how to get through and plan for that day. I knew it would just add more stress worrying about tomorrow.

Our days in active addiction were only focused on one day at a time because drinking or getting high was our only goal for the day. Doing this everyday while you were in active addiction gave us a lot of practice in focusing on one day at a time. This means we have gotten pretty damn good at it. No matter what we do we are programed to win at what we choose to do. This is the truth and is something that we must always keep in perspective. Because we can use it to our advantage.

Be Addicted To Your Recovery

So, now that we have evaluated that we are very experienced in living "One Day at a Time" in a negative way we can now switch it to allow it to better our lives.

We will always have an addictive personality, but we can now get into the mentality of being addicted to our recovery. This is a big way that I learned to get into and sustain my recovery to this day. I think about my addictive qualities as tools to help maintain and learn new ways to help strengthen my recovery. It feels absolutely amazing and it will for you too.

You see, wanting to find out how to improve your recovery as a chance to brighten your day can make you feel better than any day that you have chose to use. Learning new things about your recovery and knowing you are strengthening it has the opportunity to make you feel more euphoria than any drug you've ever taken. This is what drives my passion for recovery and can drive your recovery too.

Now that recovery is your new type of addiction here are some examples of something you can ask yourself to look for on a daily basis.

- What is a new coping skill I can learn today to put in my coping skill arsenal for when I may have a trigger?

- How can I gain something to be grateful for today?
- Where can I find a meeting to go to today?
- What is something that I can plan to talk to my counselor about when I see them next?
- Who can I make amends with today?
- What is something I can do today that I know I couldn't have done when I was using? (Going fishing, going grocery shopping without the want to spend the money on harmful things, hanging out with a specific family member, etc.)

Before you start this next chapter, you'll have to do one thing which is going to be worth it. Take it as an excuse to get outside and enjoy a nice drive or walk. This next chapter is about the Get-It-Done-Notebook. Head to the store and choose a notebook that really sticks out to you. I recommend getting a new one to represent a fresh start on life with this new tool you're going to learn. Get a pen and a marker. I say both because there is something about crossing out a goal that has been achieved with a bold black line going through it. That's just me and it works so I recommend you do it too. This will all make seance in the next chapter. Let's do this.

CHAPTER 3

Daily Goal Setting (The Get-It-Done Notebook)

If we put a fraction of the dedication that we made during our active use to our goals now, we would have zero problem reaching them.

Now that you have your notebook let's get this thing started. The Get-It-Done Notebook was made to help prioritize our goals and simplify reaching them. As soon as you get the notebook, write today's date at the top of it. Once that's done write down on today's page using bullet points all of the things that you would like to get done today, then this week, then this month. This will likely be a lot of short-term goals, but the more you have the better.

Go ahead and take a minute to write today's page down before you keep reading, I'll wait.

Ok, the benefit of this is to clear our minds of feeling like we have hundreds of things we need to get done when in all reality it's never as bad as we think. The way our minds work it is almost impossible to keep our focus on one thing if we don't write it down.

Once one thought is brought up in our heads it's replaced by something else putting it back in the back of our minds. Once it's back there and we didn't have a chance to do anything about it, we still have the feeling of worry or guilt associated with it. This feeling of guilt and worry continues to our new thought. So, we end up having all of this worry and guilt and can't even remember what caused it.

It is crucial for our minds to be as free as possible in order for us to find out what steps to take next in our lives. If we are making decisions with this guilt and worry in our minds there is a very strong chance we will be making a decision with little confidence in ourselves. Making decisions without confidence will force us to set goals we feel we may not believe we can reach. We'll hold ourselves back from setting goals we should know we are capable of.

Now that they are on paper, we can focus on them individually and they have theoretically been released from our minds. We don't have to keep putting it to the back of our heads if it's written down. So, congratulations you have made a huge step in clearing your mind. Feels a lot better right?

Being able to read it to yourself will give you new perspective on your goals and will allow you to come up with different options and choices for each goal that will more than likely keep the positivity rolling throughout your day, and life if you keep this up. As mentioned before, we often hold guilt and regret towards things that we have not achieved even though half the time we do not even remember what we are guilty about. This vicious circle keeps us in a negative mentality which makes it very difficult to reach goals confidently.

Now that each goal is written down and you can see them clearly you will find that most of them are easily achieved. (Whether you think they are easily achieved or impossible is all in your head by the way, so make the right choice). The easiest goals that only take a minute: a phone call, taking out the trash or cleaning out the closet, you have been dreading are the goals we all put off the most. At least for me it was, and still is for that matter. We put off these small goals because we tell ourselves "Well that's only going to take a second so I will do that later" then later becomes a week, and then a month and sometimes even a year. If you are in recovery or even in active addiction for that matter you understand this feeling.

Deciding to stop using drugs was our first short term goal we have been putting off for ourselves.

"I'll get clean tomorrow"

"I'll get sober when my mom brings it up again"

"I'll stop drinking after my birthday, or New Year's, or Christmas"

"I have so many other things to work on right now, I will worry about getting clean another time"

So yes, we have become very accustomed and skilled at this short-term goal procrastination. We also need to realize that we have practiced achieving short term goals very successfully during our active addiction as well. Sounds weird right? But it's very true. They were not very healthy goals, but we did achieve them. For example, during my time of active addiction I asked myself 3 questions. "Do I have any drugs left?", "How much money do I have for them if I don't?" and "How do I hustle up some money to get more". As I said these are not healthy goals but the amount of determination, I had to achieve them was remarkable.

If we put a fraction of the dedication that we made during our active use to our goals now, we would have zero problem reaching them. This is something to always keep in mind, yes more often than not our active addiction days were horrible (and if you don't think they were you are lying to yourself) but we can see a lot of positive in them. We have to. We need to see this as a learning lesson and seek out what traits we had that we can use today.

Us addicts have traits that most people either don't have or they won't be able to see things our way. These different things include empathy for those who are struggling, gratitude for just being a live today, and knowing that any possible issue we are facing is not going to be harder that it was to get sober. So, when it comes to reaching your goals know that you are strong, and you have always had the determination to do great things.

CHAPTER 4

Your Recovery
Comes First

I am proud of you because you
have chosen to be in recovery

Your recovery needs to be the absolute most important thing in your life. Without a steady and solid recovery system everything else falls apart. I was told by someone close to me something very insightful about the power of addiction and the power of choosing to use our drug of choice. They said, "You can choose one thing and lose everything else in your life, or you can lose one thing and gain everything in your life back". This is something that stuck with me and has had great meaning towards my recovery. For the best chance of success in recovery simplicity is key. You can make it as complicated as you want but it all really comes down to one phrase.

"If you don't use then everything is going to be ok."

This is where the selfish part of recovery takes place. We need to ask ourselves in every situation and when making any choice in our lives, is this going to help or hinder my life and my recovery, if you are honest about that question you are going to be just fine. This of course can be a hard decision to act on because a lot of the times the choice that will help us is something that isn't understood by others and may offend them.

Holidays make great examples for a help or hinder situation. Say you have a family Christmas party coming up and you are in the very early stages in recovery. Say you know that your family is infamous about getting very intoxicated during the family holiday party and you know it will either trigger you, or just plain annoy you the whole time your there. If we are being honest, we know that this is not the place to be for you and you know you shouldn't go. If this is the truth, then *Don't Go*. Worrying about Aunt Jane and Uncle John's feelings is not worth you taking the chance of losing your sobriety. If they are upset that you are making a decision that is going to help you in your recovery than frankly, they are not people that you want in your life anyway. Making these honest decisions is a great way to find out who to keep in your life while in early recovery and who to keep out. If you choose to keep someone out of your life during your early recovery don't worry, they will eventually come back into your life and your relationship with them will be better than it ever was before. It will be better because during this time you will have become stronger as a person and will have gained more confidence in yourself. So, in some circumstances the longer those people stay out of your life the better because every day you don't see them the stronger you will be when they come back into your life.

A lot of you that are reading this book are parents that play a big part or take full responsibility of taking care of the household. This is very important, but it is still possible to take care of our responsibilities (and others) while still putting our personal recovery first. We have to. In early recovery I made the mistake, as I'm sure a lot of us have, of worrying about making others happy before trying to do what I know made me happy and really worked for my recovery. I wondered

"What do I have to do to make my mom happy?"

"What do I do to make my dad happy?"

or "What can I do to get my girlfriend back".

What we do for one person may not be the thing that works for another. Maybe one person says you need rehab, or someone else says you need a good job and another person says you need to see a counselor. If we focus on others, we will prolong the happiness of all those around us. The one and only thing you need to keep in mind is that everyone that cares about you is saying the exact same thing…. "I just want to see them do better" or "I just want to see them be happy".

So, when we finally choose to just focus on ourselves and do what we know is working for us, we are taking care of everyone at the same time. (Que mic drop).

The power and effectiveness of choosing to be in recovery for ourselves is surreal. It simplifies everything in recovery and allows us to know what we should be proud of in our recovery. The small steps like having a week sober or even having a valid license for the first time in years may not be a big deal to others but it is a huge step for a lot of us who has let addiction take over our lives.

We should not sell ourselves short of feeling proud of these accomplishments and if you aren't getting that from anyone else, I am telling you now that I am proud of you for all that you are doing in recovery. *I am proud of you because you have chosen to be in recovery.* Even if you are in still active addiction, you have chosen to read this book, which is taking initiative to want to better your life and that is a huge step. I am also very proud of those of you who are reading this to gain an understanding of the life of recovery because you are the ones who are going to bring the understanding of addiction to life. You guys rock so keep up the good work!

That being said, not caring about what anyone thinks is extremely important too. Not caring about what anyone thinks of us gives us a great amount of freedom that can be very beneficial while in recovery.

We are the only ones that know what our realistic goals are and know what goals are going to honestly make us proud. We can achieve the goals that others make for us, and that feels good, but a lot of the times they are things that we are just doing for them so the pride of achieving them isn't that great. If we achieve the goals that we know are going to make us proud of ourselves know one else's opinions will matter. That self-pride is one of the best feelings in the world and the beauty of it is that if we do not care about whether others are proud or not, we won't be let down. Then, as we achieve our goals and keep up the good work everyone around us will start to notice. That is when we get the gratification from pleasing others. If we keep a modest lifestyle and do this recovery thing for ourselves, the feeling of someone mentioning that we are doing well, and they are proud of us makes that feeling 10 times better.

For example, from time to time my mom will ask me to help her with something and will then offer me money for helping her out. When she says this, I tell her that if she gives me money it takes away that feeling of doing something for someone else. To me that's priceless. Just a few bucks can take away that gratitude.

So, stay modest and really do this recovery thing right. You are your best motivator. This not only relates to recovery but every other aspects in life. Stop selling yourself short of gratitude towards your goals, do it for you.

CHAPTER 5

Making Amends with friends and family

There are always going to be people in our lives that we feel we need to make amends with. Some of them are going to be a lot easier than others, but it's important to deal with each of them.

There are a few different ways to handle making amends with someone. Most amends are ones that are pretty simple, mostly just apologizing for something done at a party, or something that was said. These types of amends are ones that 90% of the time the other people involved have already forgotten or didn't see it as a big deal. We tend to hold on to guilt that doesn't need to be there. So, for those little incidences, go out and make those amends.

We need to really evaluate what is being held on to in our minds that is holding us back from our confidence in recovery. It is a good idea to sit and write down all of the things that are holding you back from achieving full confidence in your recovery. What are the things that trigger your guilt about your past? Write them down so you can see all of them and decide on which one to handle first.

So many people in recovery don't do this and have held in all of these demons throughout their recovery never fully experiencing the joy of it. We need to figure out or at least begin to start to take care of our amends before this can fully happen.

Not all amends involve talking with them directly. Depending on what had happened for an amend to be considered, there are safe ways to handle them without unneeded conflict.

Sometimes bringing up a bad event from the past can be harmful for the other parties involved. This is where you bring back the question of "will this help or hinder my recovery?" but switch it to "will this help or hinder their lives?". If you feel that bringing up the past you want to make amends for will hinder them more than help them it's time to take a different approach. If you know that if the amend was made it would help them, then do it. Making amends can be just as helpful to the other party as it is for you. Most of the time they will be happy just to be a part of helping you move further in your recovery.

So how do we make amends for something we shouldn't bring up?

If you have decided that acting on an amend would hinder the other party than it's time to bring it back to you. Anything that has happened in the past you cannot change. This is something that's hard to accept but there is a way to see our mistakes in a positive light.

You were in your active addiction for the exact amount of time you needed to be for you to be sober today.

Take this to heart. If we didn't make the exact number of mistakes that we made, there is a good chance that we wouldn't be here today. A lot of amends are going to be made naturally by those who care about us. So, you focusing on your recovery and your happiness is undoubtably the best way to go.

Don't let the past get to you. You deserve to move on. You deserve to be happy. You deserve your recovery.

CHAPTER 6

Building your grain of salt (Learning to deal with others)

Staying humble is the strength in recovery.

Some of the hardest things we are going to face in our recovery are things we cannot control. We can be as strong in our recovery as possible but still be affected by other events that we had no control over.

There will be a lot of people in our lives that attempt to contact us or try and be a part of our lives that we don't want. These, as with any other negative events, are opportunities to use your skills in recovery. One of the best skills you can use in these situations is your grain of salt.

If you haven't heard of the common phrase of "taking it with a grain of salt" it means to accept something but still have a healthy level of skepticism. This can be very useful in our recovery. Taking everything that is said to us seriously can be dangerous. We need to appear that we are accepting what is being said to us while also keeping up our inner wall. With anything and everything that is said to you, prepare to take it with a grain of salt.

I have my grain of salt loaded before every interaction in life. When I hear my phone ring, before I even look at it my brain is programed to be ready for it. My brain is ready to take what is said on that phone with a grain of salt.

Most of the time it's just a common phone call from my wife asking what we want to do for dinner, but I still handle each call or interaction the same way. This puts us in the best possible position to handle bigger unexpected problems that come our way.

If we are prepared for what is going to be said to us ahead of time, we will be less likely to be affected negatively by it.

You utilize your grain of salt in physical interactions as well. For instance, if you run into someone you know in the grocery store that you're not too sure how they're going to act towards you. This is when as you are walking towards them, or they are walking towards you, you begin to build up your grain of salt. Begin your preparation to listen to them but be ready to easily subside anything negative that is said. Then you can evaluate anything negative and use it as a learning opportunity. Now you know what to expect from this person and also know that it could be said by others.

For example, when someone presents disbelief that you are going to stay in recovery. This is something that can be hard to hear in early recovery but if your grain of salt is being utilized it's something you can process. You can now expect that someone may say this ahead of time and have a better hold on dealing with it.

Know your strength

If you are doing everything you can and are confident in your work in recovery, no one else's opinion matters. There will be many people in life that may not believe you are going to stay strong. They may expect you to go back to using. They may never support you in your recovery.

One of the main things to realize when it comes to people like this is, if they are acting negatively towards you in your recovery when you have been proving yourself, they have something they are not dealing with themselves. We are easy targets for people who don't want to deal with their own issues. We give people the opportunity to say, "Well I'm not as bad as Max". So really the more they say these negative things the happier they are to have us in their lives.

When we are doing better you will find that the people who are going through the most in their lives will hit us harder with their negativity. So, when you are facing someone that is really trying their hardest to bring you down, remember that person is going through a lot that they are afraid to face. Does this sound familiar? It sounds like us. It sounds like our attitudes when people were try-ing to convince us to be sober. It sounds like us choosing to use to numb our feelings that we were too afraid to face.

So, when you are faced with someone like this, try to have a new since of understanding. No one is above anyone else. So, if anything be happy that they are lashing out at someone that has more of an understanding. You being humble and letting them know you know they are going through a lot may be the thing that changes their way of thinking for the better.

We all have issues we need to deal with that we are afraid to. Staying humble in recovery is key to a successful recovery. *Staying humble is the strength in recovery.*

CHAPTER 7

My Worst Day in Recovery vs My Best Day in Active Addiction

The worst day in my life in sobriety is by far better than my best day in active addiction. To keep those good days coming we need to put our recovery first.

I want to emphasize the meaning behind my best and worst days for a second because I have found that this is often misunderstood. The way my day is going and how I feel about each day is motivated by what is driving me that day, what my goals are, and the love I feel around me. During my active addiction my drive was to find my drug of choice, my goal was to use it, and as far as the love around me it was either absent or I did not feel I deserved it from those who wanted to show it to me.

The best days during my active addiction were those days when I successfully numbed my mental pain and covered up my emotions. This related to when I was with my "good" friends at the time, which had the same goals of numbing their pain and emotions as well. We didn't want to talk about our families and responsibilities. We didn't want to talk about the money we were spending on our alcohol or drug of choice and we didn't want to talk about the damage we were doing to our brains. Although sometimes it seemed that was an unsaid competition that I, unfortunately, was very good at.

So, you see our best days in active addiction were (or are) not really great at all. We were just successfully in denial.

Becoming more and more successful in achieving these "good days" drove us deeper into our active addictions. So, when it comes to my best days in active addiction, they weren't that great at all.

Now that I am clean and sober, I see life in a new light, and I have tools that help me with anything I need to face. No matter how rough or horrible my day is I always have my pillars of gratitude.

1. At least I remember yesterday
2. This would be so much worse if I was using
3. I can see this as a learning opportunity as I have with many problems before
4. My sobriety gives me the strength to get through anything

No matter how hard your day or life gets, if you stay in recovery you will always have these pillars with you. This is very important to remember and believe. Dealing with hard days is something we all face and as addicts they can be the most important moments in our life. Moments that pave the way for our next steps in life.

There is a reason the last stage of recovery is called maintenance. Figuring out how to deal with little stressors throughout the day is the strongest and best way to stay successful in your recovery. If we don't deal with the little things, they can grow to a point where we can't control them. This is why the one day at a time perspective is so important. If we keep ourselves happy in life and stay proud of the work we are doing, we will be able to handle whatever comes at us.

Don't sweat the small stuff, it isn't worth it.

CHAPTER 8

Spirituality

Spirituality is something that we all practice whether we realize it or not and it is very helpful in our recovery. There is a big difference between religion and spirituality. One of my most favorite sayings I've ever heard about spirituality is "Religion is for those who are afraid to go to hell and spirituality is for those who have already been there".

This quote really got to me because active addiction is a very dark place that you never want to go back to. It is, however, always there in the shadows trying to corrupt us. So that to me is the commonality of religion and spirituality. Spirituality is the ambition to stay away from the dark places we know exist. That motivation is something that can be very powerful.

We also need the ability to say "I don't know what I'm doing, I need help. Show me what to do". Being able to release all the thoughts that are burdening us to some other higher power to decide when we need it is very uplifting. Allowing some other higher power to decide when you are ready to face a specific issue or thought takes most of the pressure off you.

This does not need to be singled down to a specific higher power. I have heard many different perspectives on what a person's higher power is and the only thing that was important about them is if it worked. There is the common belief of God from a religious aspect and I've also known of someone's higher power being their cane. (Yes, their walking cane). The bottom line is that you are the one who knows what works for you spiritually and if you don't know then just say out loud "I don't know what my spirituality is, but I need your help". Maybe you'll get your answer.

Be open to trying different ideas of spirituality. We need to give ourselves the opportunity to give our stress to something or someone else from time to time.

CHAPTER 9

Vulnerability is Strength

*If we don't show vulnerability, we will
not bring our problems to light and
they will never be dealt with.*

A lot of us addicts often start down the road of addiction at a very young age. I myself started experimenting with drugs around 12 years old. One very common theory of long-term effects of drug use is that we revert to our mentality of when we decided to start altering our minds with drugs. So, when we get into recovery, we essentially are at whatever age mentality that you started to use. For me, I had a 12-year-old mentality when I first got into recovery.

Now of course we don't totally shut off our minds from all knowledge, but as far as dealing with emotions and real-life problem solving, I found this extremely true. It took me completely getting off of drugs to finally start my process of dealing with these emotions that were locked away for so many years.

When we decide to get into recovery, we are entering a whole new world. Change is very intimidating when we have been training our brains to do the same thing everyday for such a long time. We need to be able to talk about all of the things that we are not comfortable with and in order to do this we need to practice vulnerability.

You may see vulnerability as a weakness, but this is very far from the truth. If you are choosing to hold in your emotions because of false pride you are holding yourself back from mental and emotional growth. Whether you want to admit it or not you admire those who are comfortable asking for help and showing vulnerability. *If we don't show vulnerability, we will not bring our problems to light and they will never be dealt with.* These are the cold hard facts and it's something you need to embrace to prove to yourself that you are strong in your recovery.

It's alright to not know what to do, there are a lot of people who can help. If we don't bring our problems to light, we may have the danger of learning to cope with it in an unhealthy way. This will inevitably lead us back to using. This is why vulnerability and asking for help is so important.

Wanting to help others is something that feels really good for an addict and helping others is what keeps us sober. So, when you are asking someone for help, you're genuinely helping them strengthen their recovery too. This goes for friends, loved ones and counselors too. We all feel very good when we get a chance to help others. So go make someone's day and ask for help.

CHAPTER 10

Love your mistakes

*The strongest people are the ones who ask
for help and look forward to learning*

Mistakes are one of the things I look forward to most when it comes to my recovery, and it needs to be yours too. There is no way to get around making mistakes from time to time. So, choosing to see the positive in them is the way to go.

If we don't make mistakes, we don't have the chance to learn from them. When you come to a point, or maybe you are already there, when you have a pretty strong hold on your recovery you may start to get complacent. This can get very bad.

I often admire those in early recovery because they are going through so many battles that are building that proud recovery. As I've said before I admire those in that first year in recovery more than those with a decade. That is when we work the hardest in our recovery and fight the hardest battles. Again, if you are in your first year of recovery, You Rock.

If we make a mistake it gives us a chance to reevaluate our recovery and we have that chance to make it even stronger. This never stops and that is a beautiful thing. Knowing that we will always have chances to strengthen our recovery is really the foundation of being a proud addict.

Knowing we won't be able to fully trust ourselves and we will always face personal battles is what makes us warriors in this recovery. *The strongest people are the ones who ask for help and look forward to learning.*

Remember that.

You're not responsible for your first thought.
You're responsible for your second.

One of the main things to remember is our addictive mind is always going to be there trying to throw us off our game. It is important to not get discouraged about a bad thought or trigger that pops in your head. That first thought is something that we are never going to be able to control, and that's ok.

Our first thoughts are a reaction to our impulsive mentality that we thrived on during our active addiction. Our addictive mind will always remember that, so when that trigger or unhealthy thought pops in your head it happens without warning. This is when the second thought comes into play.

Recovery gives us the power of having a second thought and our second thought is what we have total control over.

For example, from time to time I happen to pass by a local liquor store that I used to go to very often when I was drinking. Sometimes when I drive past my first thoughts will come into play and I find myself forming a plan for a relapse.

How much money do I have?

How many shots can I take without people knowing I'm drunk?

Where can I hide it when I get home?

How much will I need to get me through the next couple days?

These thoughts happen almost instantly and without warning. At first, I was discouraged to have these thoughts. This is a normal feeling at first, especially if we are doing good in our recovery. Now when they happen, I just laugh and almost find it amusing. If we are not going to be able to stop them, we have to find an attitude to counter act any negative vibes.

See these events as a new way to learn what your possible triggers might be. You should actually look forward to them because of this. Anyway, to find out a way to find your triggers is a great thing and with these thoughts coming with no effort, you got it made.

Keep that second thought simple by using the Help or Hinder Method. If you stick to this, it will make things simple and easier to evaluate. When that trigger hits while driving by the liquor store, I ask myself "Will this help or hinder my recovery?" it's a pretty clear answer, obviously hinder.

Even though the answer seems obvious our addictive mind will still try to convince us with rationalization. This is why it is good to have a plan for when these thoughts happen. Calling someone that you can trust, playing a specific song, or grabbing a coin that helps you remember your sobriety is number one. These are some great second thoughts that you should try out for yourself.

Everybody's way to cope with that first thought will be different. It is important to find out what works for you. Think about things that you really like to do, and you find enjoyment in. Focus on honesty in knowing what you know will keep you out of that first thought mentality. These are the things that are going to be a huge help in your recovery.

So, embrace that second thought, and let go of your first. You got this.

CHAPTER 11

Judgement, One Thing You Need to Win

If we are not being judged by others during our times of self-improvement and recovery, we are not moving in the right direction.

Let's face it, there are a lot of people in this world that do not have the ambition to live life in a new and more positive way. Therefore, if you are choosing to take a new path (which if you are reading this, you are) this may make others uncomfortable and begin to judge you for it. This is extremely true for us addicts facing the number of different levels of judgment in how people see us in recovery. If you are someone who is trying to gain a better understand of what recovery is about, the subject of judgment will really help put things in perspective.

Learning to let go of the stigma of addiction and addicts being bad people is key to being proud of your choice of changing your way of life. If you are early in your recovery you are probably facing a lot of judgement right now, whether it be from family, using friends that are mad that you're not using any more, or just a random person that heard you used to use. To be 100% honest with you, this is never going to end, even after having years in recovery I still have others that judge me for being an addict.

For me this is an absolutely beautiful thing and it will be for you to.

People that are judging you are just proof that you are moving in the right direction, so in all reality *it is a compliment*. I say bring on the judgement and you should too. This may be uncomfortable and hard to grasp at first but remember, if changing your life in recovery was easy it wouldn't be worth the work. Any path that is easy in recovery is more than likely the wrong way. Embrace the judgement of others because it is a sign that you are doing the right thing.

The more judgement you face the more likely you are moving in the right direction. Think about it. When you see celebrities that are successful and have all this money do you feel envious? Do you look for their flaws to make your envy less intense? If you are saying no, you're lying. It's all good but now it's time to be honest.

We all naturally judge someone within seconds of seeing them. It's normal to feel this way and it can be a good way to find out what goals we would like to set for ourselves.

Now that we have addressed that we judge others before we even realize it, we can now see how we can use it to benefit our recovery. This goes back to the "You're not responsible for your first thought, your responsible for your second thought".

Ask yourself "Am I judging this person harshly?" and "Am I going to let this person get to me?".

Get to a point in your recovery that both of the answers to these questions are no and you'll continue on your track of successful recovery.

CHAPTER 12

Recovery's Armageddon

Armageddon… this term is intimidating, but it is an opportunity to prepare to conquer an inner battle. What I mean by this is as long as I have been in recovery, working as a chemical dependency counselor, and even towards the end of my active addiction, I have noticed that right when someone chooses to get into recovery they face a certain day where everything seems to go wrong. Call it destiny, call it karma, call it whatever you want, it will and always happens to everyone in recovery.

This day, for example, you stub your toe in the morning, then accidently cut yourself shaving, then you find out you got in trouble at your job for something you didn't do, then traffic is horrible, then you hear a family member passed away, then you find out someone you didn't even think about contacts you about something you did in the past. All in the same day. This of course will be different for everybody happening in different levels of intensity, but it always happens.

So, what do we do about it? Well, we prepare, we train ourselves, and become aware that Recovery's Armageddon is coming. We prep ourselves by building up coping skills. Coping skills are the brick walls of our recovery. When I say this, I mean that before a certain event gets to a point that we have a trigger, it has to break through all of our coping skills that we have built to block it. Every coping skill we have is a layer of resistance for a trigger to attempt to break through. So, build those coping skills.

Be prepared for your Recovery's Armageddon. The more we prep for it and expect it to be very impactful, the less intense it will actually be. Think of it like when you were a kid getting a booster shot and it was going to be the worst pain in the world. All of that preparation set your mind to prepare for that pain. Then of course when you get it done it's nowhere near what you prepared for.

If you see your Recovery's Armageddon in this light you will be in good shape. You should look forward to it! Recovery's Armageddon is a huge opportunity to prove your strength in your recovery.

CHAPTER 13

Friends and Family

Genetics holds the gun and environment pulls the trigger. Did you know that a child born with parents that have an addiction is four times more likely to become addicted themselves? This is something that scared the shit out of me when I first learned about it. It made me feel nervous about my children growing up and facing the same thing I faced in my active addiction, but for those of you who are parents don't worry, there is a silver lining to this. If our children do start to show signs of addiction, we are undoubtably equipped with some of the best advice we could give someone who might be struggling with addiction.

You know your kids better than anyone else and you will have your own ways of parenting, but here is what I plan on doing. I am choosing to refrain from telling my kids anything other than I just don't drink or use drugs until the day that I hear the magic words "Dad you just don't get it!". In a weird way I am very excited about this day because it will happen. There is no way around it. If you are in denial about this then give yourself a reality check.

Now this is my opinion, yours may be different. As with everything in this book I am just providing a different perspective on things. This is what works for me.

I feel that allowing them to start to make their own mistakes without me forcing unwanted advice is the best key to giving advice to kids. Now if you don't have kids this works for anyone younger in your family or friends asking advice about what to do because they know you have been through it.

Friends are important in life. We need friends. So how do we choose who's a good friend?

I will say that in the very beginning when we are first introduced to drugs or alcohol it is a bonding moment with our peers. It is an innocent thing. We all choose to use but none of us choose to become an addict. We don't choose to become addicted. We found it very easy to ignore the warning signs of early addiction because we had so many people around us providing an astounding amount of rationalization.

Once the responsible friends that may not have a problem begin to cut down or stop using, they tend to go down a different road without us. We of course cannot blame them for this because I know for me, I wouldn't have wanted to be around me either, but we then feel lost because we are sunk into a mental headlock of needing this drug of choice that has been rationalized for so long.

We then search for others that will understand, other active addicts and you can play the tape out from there.

So how do we gain friends now?

When it comes to friend it is quality over quantity. Having one or two very close friends to go to for anything is way more effective than 100 that only care if there is something in it for them. To be honest having 100 friends sounds exhausting anyway. We only need a few to keep us afloat and happy.

I recommend in early recovery finding someone who has an extensive time in recovery or has a strong understanding of it. Whether or not they understand it or not can be very crucial for us.

I have a very simple technique for finding out if a person would be a good friend while in recovery and if you go by it honestly you will be good. Just ask yourself in your head what their answer would be if you asked them

"Hey, I really just want to have one more drink/just use one more time and be done. Would you just keep that between us?"

If their answer would be yes, then you need to go separate ways. If they say no and possibly want to kick your ass for even saying that, they are a good advocate for friendship. If you are not sure of what they would say just stick with the people that you know would answer no until you get a better feel for them.

When To Give Advice or Help Someone In Early Recovery

Waiting for the right time to give advice to someone is extremely important for both you and the one you are planning to give advice to. Think about what you would say to someone who is giving you advice while you were in your active addiction. I know for me I hated it and wanted to do the exact opposite of what they were telling me to do. This is very important to remember when you are dealing with someone you feel needs to hear your advice.

The best thing to do is keep it simple. Let them know that you care about them and if they need help, they can come to you. This way it is totally on them to decide when they are ready to make a change in their life. Once someone comes to you, lead them to someone else until you are ready.

This could be someone in AA with a longer time in recovery, giving them a contact number to get into treatment, or going to a meeting with them and then going separate ways after the meeting. Always meet someone that is either in active addiction or early recovery in a neutral place. Never meet at each other's house or anywhere in public where you can possibly run into unpredictable situations.

Explain these rules very clearly to whoever you are thinking about helping before you choose to help them. If they are offended by these rules and are making a fuss about it, they are not ready. Accept this, stand your ground and cut ties with them. When they are truly ready you will be the one that they knew had the right idea all along.

This is a situation where the longer they are out of your life, the stronger you will have become and more likely to have the credibility to give advice. So, focusing on your own recovery is the best way to help anyone else.

The best way to help someone is to prove it can be done.

CHAPTER 14

Becoming A Lighthouse of Recovery

*The best way to help someone is
to prove it can be done.*

What traits do you think of when you think of a light-house? A light house is built to be strong, built to last forever, and to shine bright for others to see. Focusing these traits on recovery is something that will be very effective and useful in your recovery, mainly when it comes to helping others.

First off, in this metaphor the beacon of light represents a signal for others that you are willing and ready to help, keep that in mind.

Before the light is even thought of being attached, a structure needs to be constructed. This is the same thing as building your strong foundation in your recovery. You are also building this foundation with the expectation of waves hitting hard against your foundation which can make building the foundation much more difficult.

These waves in your recovery could be many different things like triggers, negativity, judgment, using friends, and whatever else may possibly hold you back from keeping a positive mentality in your recovery. Just remember each of these waves is going to make you prouder of your success and in what you have built, so bring them on.

A light house is not built all at once, it is built one stone at a time. To create the strongest possible lighthouse, you will need to place each stone perfectly as you go along.

One...Stone...At...A...Time... Sound familiar? This is that part that represents one day at a time. If you are not focused solely on making today the best, the likelihood that the days to follow are unproductive is twice as likely.

If one stone is placed wrong, all the stones that follow are going to be off as well. Don't rush things, you have plenty of time to get this done.

Let's fast forward to looking at the strong foundation you have built. You are so proud of the time you took to make it as strong as you could, and you have taken all the waves that came at you like a champ. Now it is time to place that beacon on your lighthouse. As mentioned before, this beacon represents a signal for others that you are willing and ready to help. You are confident and willing to help others.

One of the most important traits of a lighthouse is it remains in one place and never moves. In recovery this means that what you have built needs to remain consistent with yourself. The rules you have made for yourself that are working to keep you sober need to stay your foundation. If you truly stick to what works, you'll stay strong.

Now, the others who are looking for help are represented by the ships that are looking for a safe place to rest until they are ready to build a lighthouse of their own. They see your powerful beacon from a rough sea and move closer to witness the strong structure that you have built to keep you strong.

You are allowing them to study what you have done and can teach them the skills you have learned to keep you strong in your recovery. All this advice is given with the intention of them learning these skills and then returning to sea to use them for themselves. The longer they stay, the more comfortable they will be with relying on you for safety and security. The longer they stay, the longer it will take them to learn that this needs to be done on their own for it to work. Don't waste your time and don't waste theirs. Give them the advice they need and send them on their way. *The best way to help someone is to prove it can be done.*

This is what it means to be a lighthouse in recovery.

CHAPTER 15

The Bowl of Cereal (Every day is a gift, that's why it's called the present)

The first few months of my recovery were not very convincing for me. I didn't understand what the big deal was when it came to this recovery thing. I wasn't having fun and didn't see the benefits of not being in active addiction. I knew that it was supposed to be a lot better than when I was using but I didn't see why recovery was such a better option. It wasn't until I woke up one morning and made the very simple decision of having a bowl of cereal when it all hit me.

I looked down at my bowl of frosted flakes with ice cold milk and sugar sprinkled over the top and my heart sunk into my chest. I wasn't hungover, I wasn't withdrawing, and I was not focused solely on my drug of choice for survival. I realized that it had been years since I had been able to just have a bowl of cereal. Just the thought of milk during my active addiction was probably one of the most unappealing things I could think of.

My only thought when I woke up during my active addiction was how much do I have left and/or how do I get more. These simple questions ruled my life and were the only two questions that mattered to me. It wasn't until these two questions where irrelevant that my life truly took a huge turn in the right direction.

An addict's drug of choice has such power over an them that it comes down to the simple perspective of choosing one thing and losing everything else or getting rid of the one thing and gaining everything back in your life. As mentioned earlier in the book.

This is one of the most accurate perspectives that I've practiced when it comes to how addiction effects one's life. The power of only having to decide on whether this one thing is going to be in your life or not. This one thing, to drastically alter the chance of having either a remarkably happy life or crippling despair and possible death.

This is something that is very hard to see when in active addiction but when it is brought to light can really help put things in perspective.

Gratitude plays a big role in this perspective and gratitude can be very hard to notice in early recovery. We often feel that we don't deserve to be grateful for anything in early recovery because of the mistakes we've made. I'm here to tell you, you do.

We all deserve to feel the powerful benefits that gratitude has to offer. Practice gratitude. You're alive today, so enjoy that bowl of cereal.

CHAPTER 16

Dealing with guilt

Guilt is like a virus and the vaccine is keeping it simple.

Guilt is something that pops into our heads from time to time during the day that holds us back from fully enjoying the things we should. Guilt surprises us right when we are close to our breaking point of feeling confident in our lives.

It would happen for me right before I would start to enjoy my favorite TV show. I'd think about relaxing on the couch all day excited about my personal time and then right when I hit play for the show my mind tells me "You don't deserve to enjoy this show. You could have done so much more today, and you have to deal with all this stuff from your past". Then I would turn off the TV and sit in disgust.

This is how I used to deal with guilt but now things have changed. Feeling guilt is an honest and normal thing and there will always be things we feel guilty about. The goal, however, is to knock out the big things first so that the small feelings of guilt become easier to manage.

The small feelings of guilt more than likely will come throughout your day in your head. The larger and heavier feelings of guilt always hit right before bed, keeping us awake with anxiety. It never fails, but there is a beauty in guilt.

Guilt is actually something to look forward to!

This book is all about finding the positive in things and guilt conveniently brings our problems to light. Looking forward to our problems is the best way to take them head on. If we are ready for them, we can have a plan to learn from them. With guilt coming into our heads naturally we don't have to search for things to learn from. They are right there in front of us.

I have found it more helpful to just be ready for moments of guilt rather than sitting down and evaluating what you could feel guilty about. "What you could feel guilty about" being the main issue. If we look back and choose things to be guilty about rather than dealing with it when it happens, we will more than likely come up with things that we don't even need to feel guilty about.

Guilt is like a virus and the vaccine is keeping it simple. Keep it simple and let these things happen naturally. They will come into play when it's time. No need to sulk on it all now. Just focus on you, stay positive and keep your head held high.

CHAPTER 17

The Journal Perspective

Keeping a journal is something that I recommend everyone to at least try once in their lives. Journaling has a lot of helpful qualities for self-evaluation and insight on goal setting.

When I suggest anyone to try out journaling I try and keep it basic. Write just once in the morning and once at night. I'll also tell them to just keep it simple. Just write what's on your mind right when you get up. Then write what's going on in your mind before going to sleep.

You will be surprised about what you write down. It's very hard to have a full perspective on our emotions when we have a lot going on in our minds. We always feel them but writing them down is a whole different story.

The idea is to be able to visualize what is going on in our heads.

Once you have started writing in your journal for a few days it will help you to change your thought process. You'll begin to start analyzing your decisions throughout the day because you know that you are going to have to write about it later in the night.

Even if you do not have a journal ask yourself "Would I be happy writing about this in my journal tonight?".

If you do not ask someone else and only ask yourself a question you are the only person that can judge yourself. You are the only one who truly knows if you are lying or not. So, when you ask yourself "would I be happy writing about this in my journal tonight?" you are putting yourself into the mentality of how you feel about your day before you go to bed.

You can use this for any type of situation. It could be anything from deciding if you want a candy bar that you know you shouldn't have, to wondering how to tell someone their loved one has passed away. No matter what situation you're in you can ask yourself this same question. It's a perfect example of keeping it simple and yet allowing all your emotions to be involved.

If you keep the question in your head "Would I be happy writing about this in my journal tonight?", you're golden.

Try journaling for 2 weeks to get a full experience of it and see if it's something you want to continue. You will at least get the experience of what you would write down naturally throughout the day. I still write in mine today.

CHAPTER 18

Relationships

Should you be in a relationship in early recovery? No. You are your one and only when it comes to your recovery.

In order to be successful in recovery we need to find out who we are, how we feel about ourselves, and feel that we deserve a positive and healthy relationship.

During our active addiction it is very common to have only people around us that support our unproductive and destructive behavior because face it, none of us want to be judged for what we are choosing to do in life. This is the reason why people that are healthy for us in life and the people we love kind of dwindle off and give us more space.

This absolutely falls under those who don't have addictions and are just in a rut in life not motivated to do much as well. Overall, we need to find ourselves and become the person that we feel deserves someone great that loves us for who we are.

I emphasize again, *you need to become someone that you feel deserves a happy and healthy relationship.* Until you find yourself and build enough confidence, staying away from a committed relationship is your best bet.

See it as you are the one that is in a fresh new relationship with yourself. Ask yourself questions about what you like to do in your spare time? What are your goals in life? What are your favorite movies? What are things you wish you could be better at that you feel could really benefit your life?

For me, I really had no idea what the answer to all these questions were. My only hobby was drinking, that's it.

When it came to thinking of anything other than drinking or using whatever drug of choice it was at the time, discovering new hobbies was not a priority. Once we are sober and our mind clears a little, we are able to evaluate these things. If we don't find these things out for ourselves before we begin to look for someone else to be with, our focus will be on them and finding these things won't be a priority anymore.

Finding your self is a beautiful thing! You are an amazing person that deserves someone who cares about you and will treat you well. Say these statements below to yourself out loud right now.

"Finding myself is a beautiful thing"

"I am an amazing person"

"I deserve some one that truly cares about me"

"I am strong".

Now say them again a little louder. (Go ahead I'll wait) Say them as many times as you need to until you feel the adrenaline of the realization of what you just discovered. I am not joking when I say this. Sometimes we need to be over the top in stating these kinds of things to really get them.

Saying these things regularly will help out a lot. A great time to do it is in the morning in the mirror. It's also a good idea to do it before bed. Confidence is key in bettering our lives and keeps us in the best place for sustaining a successful recovery.

What to look for when it's time to start a relationship

We need someone who is going to understand we are illogical.

I say this because there are many things involved with recovery that is illogical. We need someone that will be ok with leaving any situation right away when needed with no question. In early recovery we often face social situations that we know we need to leave. This is actually the main question to focus on when we begin to look for someone.

"Would this person be ok with leaving without question if I have a trigger?"

If you ask yourself this question honestly and stick to your gut feeling with the answer, you have a good shot at a healthy relationship.

When you get to a point in your life where you have truly found yourself and you feel confident in your recovery, you can start pondering the idea of a relationship.

For the record, I don't recommend looking for one right away. The stronger you get in your recovery the higher your chances are for having a lasting relationship. So, take your time.

Some of the key things to look for when choosing a significant other while in recovery are honesty, loyalty, open-mindedness, and being motivated to bettering themselves. Most importantly it needs to be someone that understands recovery and knows that it comes first over anything else.

These traits are all key in a healthy relationship and you need to believe you deserve someone with all of them. There is no need to sell yourself short of anything less than total happiness when it comes to being in a successful relationship. You have worked very hard to be where you are in your recovery and you deserve someone that will support you and motivate you to continue bettering your life.

You also are going to want someone who is dedicated to motivating themselves as well. Someone that is willing and open minded to what you have to say and is willing to take what you say to heart, even if it's something they don't want to hear. This is where the open-mindedness comes in and is crucial in helping us to continue to strengthen our recovery. If we get upset about what someone is saying and/or calling us out on, we know that is what we need to work on most. Remember that.

One of the most important things to remember about being in a relationship is to always remain independent as a person. The best relationships are the ones that can end with minimal emotional turmoil and there is still confidence on both sides that their lives will go on.

Being financially independent is important too. You need to limit as many material and emotional assets that will hold you back from moving on if things aren't going well.

Don't just settle and decide to stay together because you're comfortable and are nervous to move on. This is why so many people who aren't happy or in love stay married for years. They resent each other but financially they are stable and just the thought of bringing up something negative like divorce isn't worth the stress.

The amount of restrictions you have on your life when this is going on is unbelievable. If you are not happy together you are not going to push each other to improve yourselves. If we aren't improving our lives what are we even doing? It's a waste of time and for us addicts, if we are not continuing to strengthen our recovery and achieve our goals our chance of relapse goes up. So, if you are in a relationship now that you feel is unhealthy and you know you'd be happier if you left it. Do what you have to do and start that process.

We need to be bold when it comes to our recovery. We have to be able to cut someone out of our lives if they are going to hinder our recovery. One of the most impactful and accurate things my mom has ever said to me is the common phrase "You are who you hang out with". This could not be further from the truth.

Whoever you are around all the time is who you are going to become. So, when it comes to relationships you better be sure you want to be just like them.

CHAPTER 19

Building Your Barrier

You often hear from others in recovery that we need to build a barrier towards those that may be unhealthy in our recovery. I know for myself there were A LOT of people that I needed to build a barrier for. It can be mentally exhausting trying to think of every single person we need to build a barrier for.

My solution to this was instead of choosing who I would build an individual barrier for I chose to only build a barrier around myself. If we build a strong wall around ourselves, we don't have to deal with deciding on who to specifically build a barrier for.

That being said, we all have those people who we know a barrier is needed; unhelpful family members, drug dealers, and if they are enabling us even our parents. Everybody's recovery is different. So, the best advice I can give you is to build up a strong personal barrier. Deal with who you need to stay away from when the event presents itself.

It is best to not worry about the things in the future that we have no control over. The more you worry about the future the less you can focus on the present. If you keep worrying all day the only thing you can guarantee will happen is that you're going to be upset that you worried all day.

This is the best way to help you build your strong personal barrier. Don't worry about who you are going to run into or who you need to build barriers around. Focus on your inner strength and face them when they present themselves to you.

This does not have to just be a physical barrier it is social as well. With social media today and the internet being so prominent we do most of our communicating digitally. When you get a message from someone online that is when they have hit your barrier. This is the time where you decide to either let them in or be sure they stay out. A simple way for controlling social media is to block those people that we don't want to talk to.

Build that personal barrier strong until you are proud of the amount of strength it can hold. You got this.

CHAPTER 20

Maintenance

You chose a life of recovery

Now is the time to evaluate everything you've learned and put together the arsenal that will defend your recovery for the long run. Maintenance is the last stage of the stages of change and states that it should be practiced your whole life in recovery. For me this is the best part of recovery.

We have gone through so much in our lives that could and did bring us to points where we didn't believe we could have made it out of, but we did. *You chose a life of recovery.* You chose to become clean and sober, and if you haven't you have at least opened your mind to a life in recovery because you are reading this book. You should be proud of that.

We will never end this fight with our addictive minds. We will never not face triggers and urges to use our drug of choice. We will always face obstacles to where our sobriety is challenged throughout our entire life. If you do not see this as an amazing opportunity for life, keep reading.

You are a warrior. You have earned the right to be proud of the work you have done and the life you have given yourself in recovery. You now have the chance to prove that to yourself every day, which really is amazing.

A lot of people have relapsed just because of a little stressor they have faced that day and not even a big life changing event. This is why maintaining your stability in recovery during everyday small stressors is so important. When a big life changing event happens to someone they are put to the ultimate test in their recovery and we need to be as prepared as possible. How do we prepare for that?

We focus on building our happiness and productivity in life one day at a time. That is how we prepare ourselves. If we stop motivating ourselves to continue to work hard in our recovery and sustain inner happiness, we are making it a much harder battle then it has to be.

Focusing on making today, *just today*, the best day it can be and focusing on not letting today get to you gives you more strength than anything else in your recovery. If you continue to build your confidence and live by your rules of recovery daily, you will become stronger with every day. As I am typing this now, I have been sober for over 5 years and I can promise you that every day in my recovery has always been better than my last.

This is the beauty of maintenance. If you focus on maintaining your successful recovery you will feel that same feeling of joy in early recovery every single day.

So, maintain your passion of becoming proud of who you were meant to be every day.

The Ground Rules: This is it

These ground rules are the key to sustaining maintenance and a successful recovery. If you stick to these ground rules and truly live by them, I promise you, you will live a full life of sobriety.

1. Be honest

Being honest with ourselves is the key to making any decision in our lives. Every... Single... Decision... Honesty... Honesty.... Honesty. If you are not ready to practice complete honesty, you need to reevaluate your recovery. That's just being honest.

This rule is also the foundation for all of the other ground rules. So again, this is very, very important.

2. Do not trust yourself

One of the most naive things you can do in your recovery is say the words "I got this". Now don't get me wrong I am all about confidence in your recovery, but confidence and complacency are very, very close together. We need to have a little distrust in ourselves when it comes to our ability to stay clean and sober in any event. Be proud of your modesty toward knowing that you are fighting a daily battle that you intend to win. *Don't underestimate the assertiveness of our addictive minds.*

3. Have outside recovery in your life

It is important to always have some sort of outside recovery in your life. A lot of times when people complete their treatment, they stop surrounding themselves with recovery, then they wonder why they fall back into their old ways. Without outside assistance helping us remember our training in recovery we lose it. Outside recovery can be anything from going to a meeting every day to just meeting with someone else in recovery for coffee once a month. Either way, you have something to look forward to that keeps your mind on recovery.

4. Strive for happiness

This is the last and most important ground rule. *Happiness is the answer to everything, and honesty is what brings us true happiness.* We can be a part of tons of things that we think makes us happy but until we are truly honest, we won't reach true happiness.

Any negative event that happens strive to regain your happiness. When you feel very happy strive to find out how to make that happiness grow. Never stop striving for happiness. Be proud of your recovery. Be proud of who you were meant to be and reach those goals you were meant to achieve.

That's it. It's all you now. **Take this world by the horns.**

CPSIA information can be obtained
at www.ICGtesting.com
Printed in the USA
LVHW040805170622
721514LV00017B/1270